# This book belongs to

_____

_____

# EASTER MAZES
# FOR KIDS AGES 8-12

D1737530

## Copyright © 2023

PUZZLE # 1

PUZZLE # 2

PUZZLE # 3

PUZZLE # 4

PUZZLE # 5

PUZZLE # 6

PUZZLE # 7

PUZZLE # 8

PUZZLE # 9

PUZZLE # 10

PUZZLE # 11

PUZZLE # 12

PUZZLE # 13

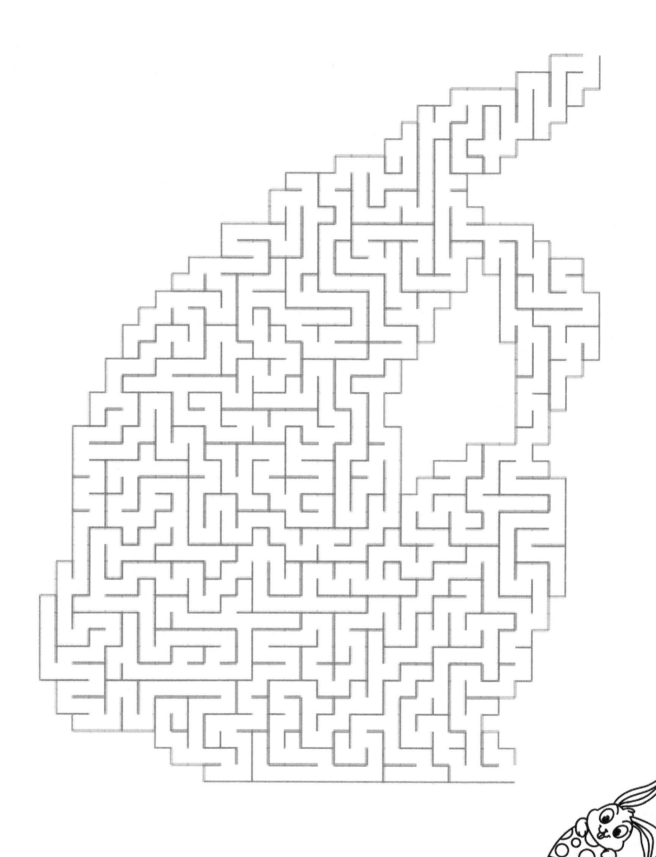

PUZZLE # 14

PUZZLE # 15

PUZZLE # 16

PUZZLE # 17

PUZZLE # 18

PUZZLE # 19

PUZZLE # 20

PUZZLE # 21

PUZZLE # 22

PUZZLE # 23

PUZZLE # 24

PUZZLE # 25

PUZZLE # 26

PUZZLE # 27

PUZZLE # 28

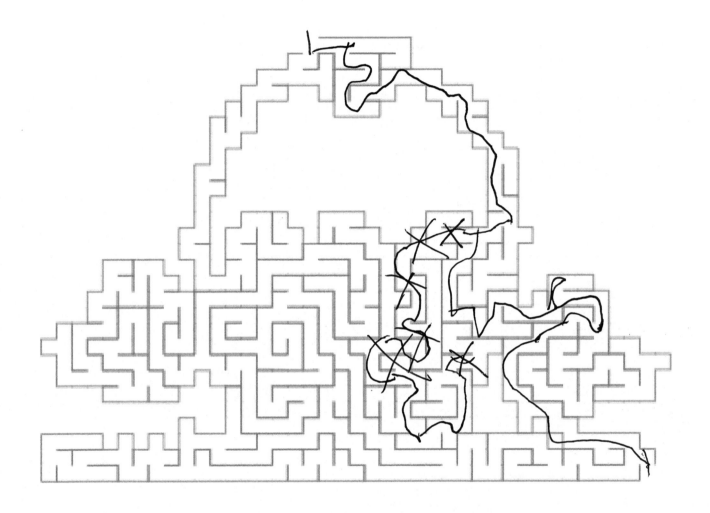

PUZZLE # 29

PUZZLE # 30

PUZZLE # 31

PUZZLE # 32

PUZZLE # 33

PUZZLE # 34

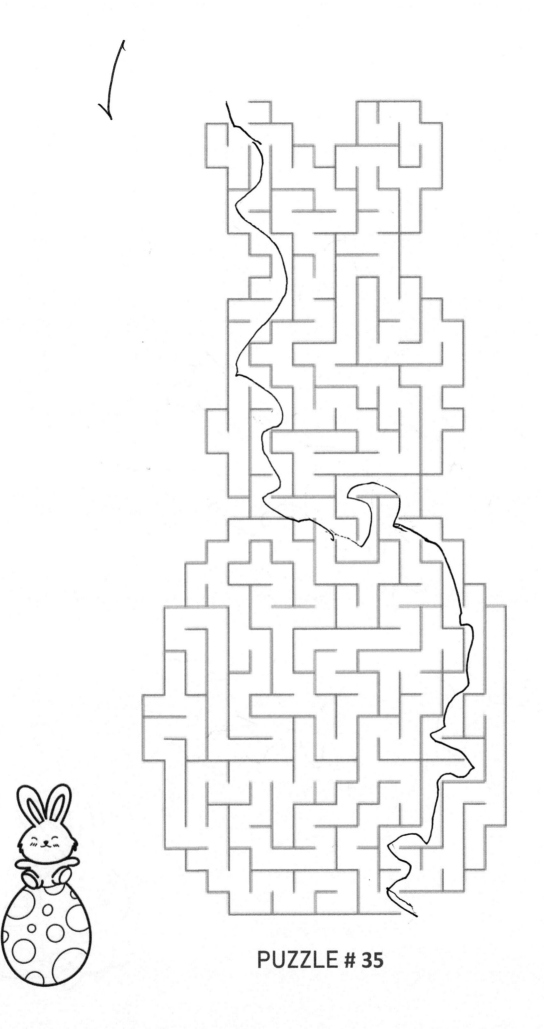

PUZZLE # 35

PUZZLE # 36

PUZZLE # 37

PUZZLE # 38

PUZZLE # 39

PUZZLE # 40

# SOLUTIONS

PUZZLE # 1

PUZZLE # 2

PUZZLE # 3

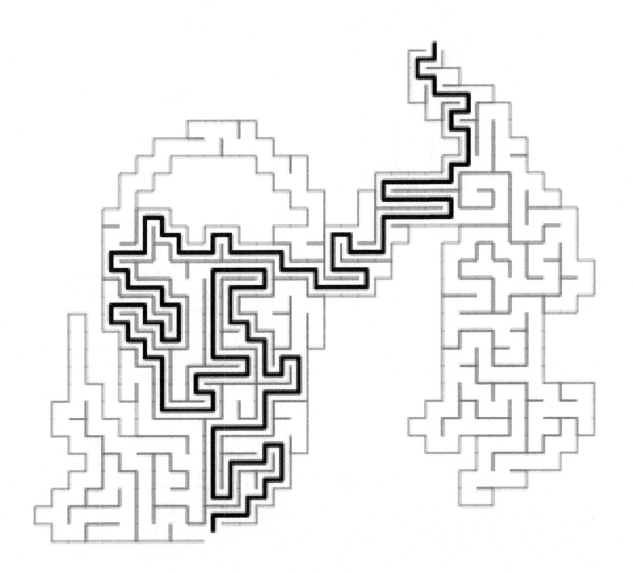

PUZZLE # 4

PUZZLE # 5

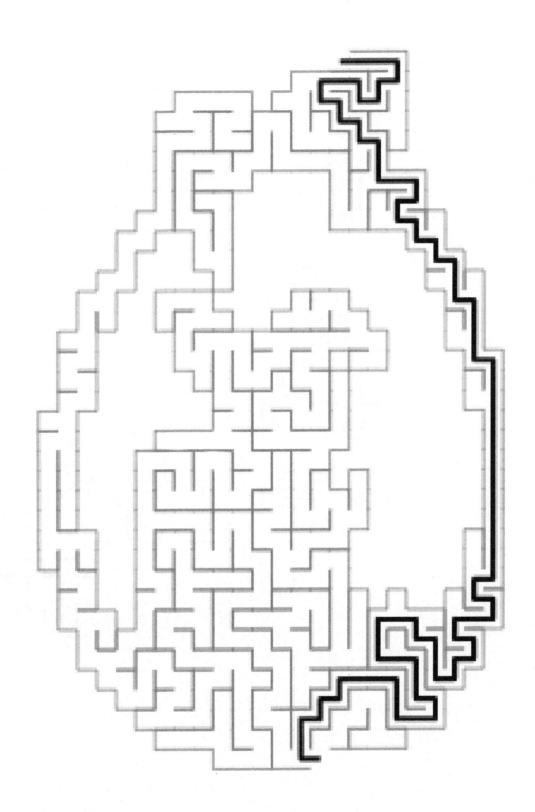

PUZZLE # 6

PUZZLE # 7

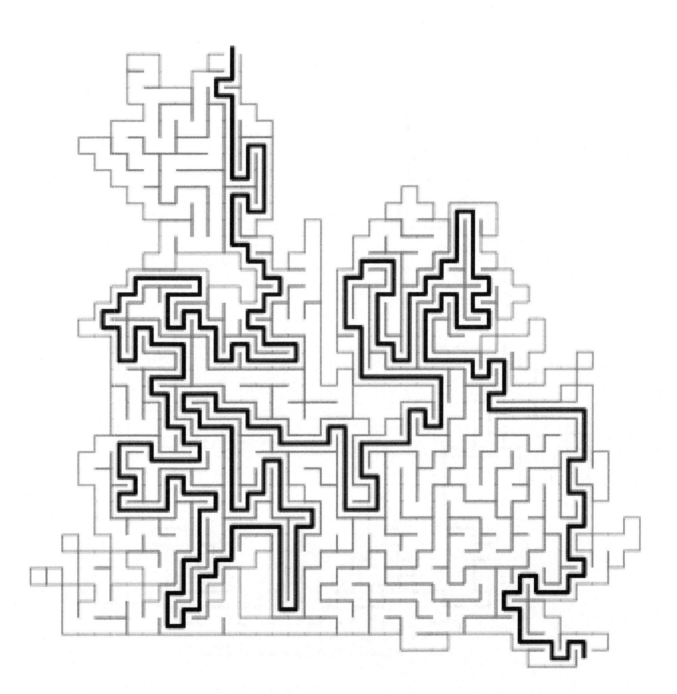

PUZZLE # 8

PUZZLE # 9

PUZZLE # 10

PUZZLE # 11

PUZZLE # 12

PUZZLE # 13

PUZZLE # 14

PUZZLE # 15

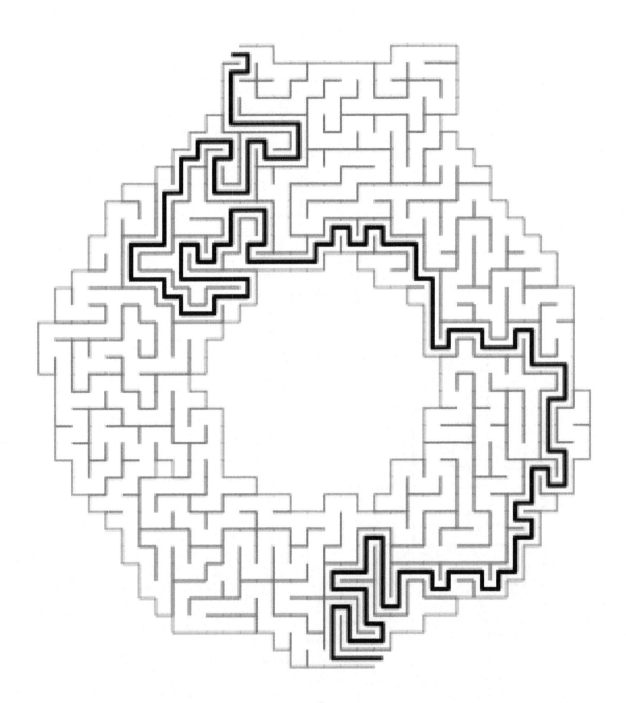

PUZZLE # 16

PUZZLE # 17

PUZZLE # 18

PUZZLE # 19

PUZZLE # 20

PUZZLE # 21

PUZZLE # 22

PUZZLE # 23

PUZZLE # 24

PUZZLE # 25

PUZZLE # 26

PUZZLE # 27

PUZZLE # 28

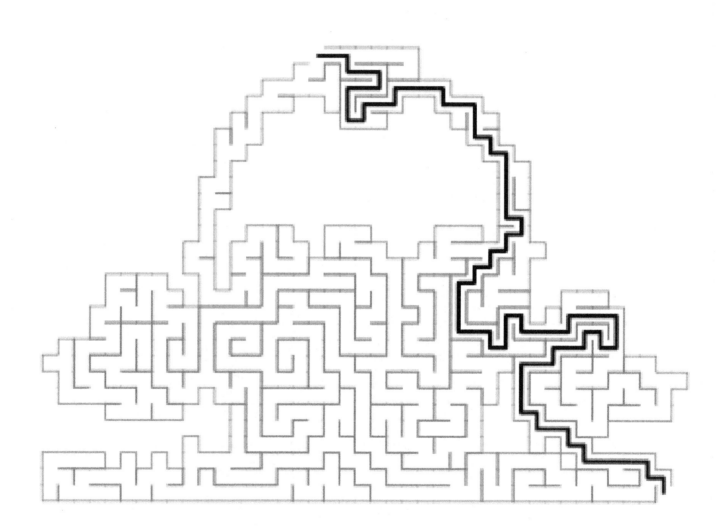

PUZZLE # 29

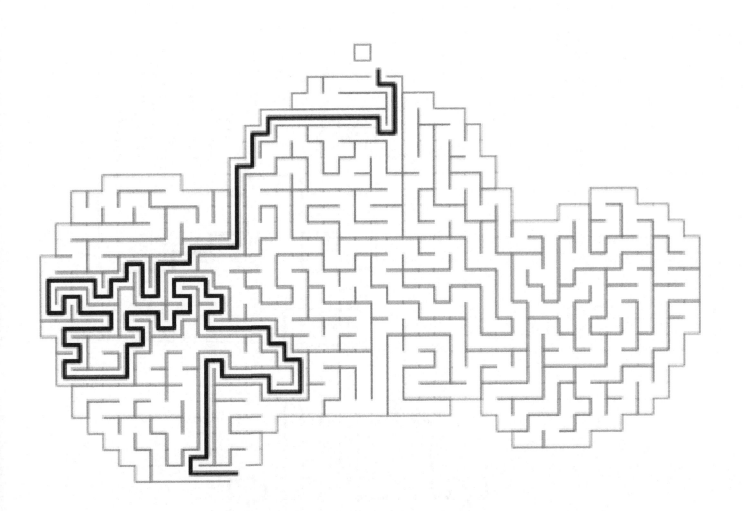

PUZZLE # 30

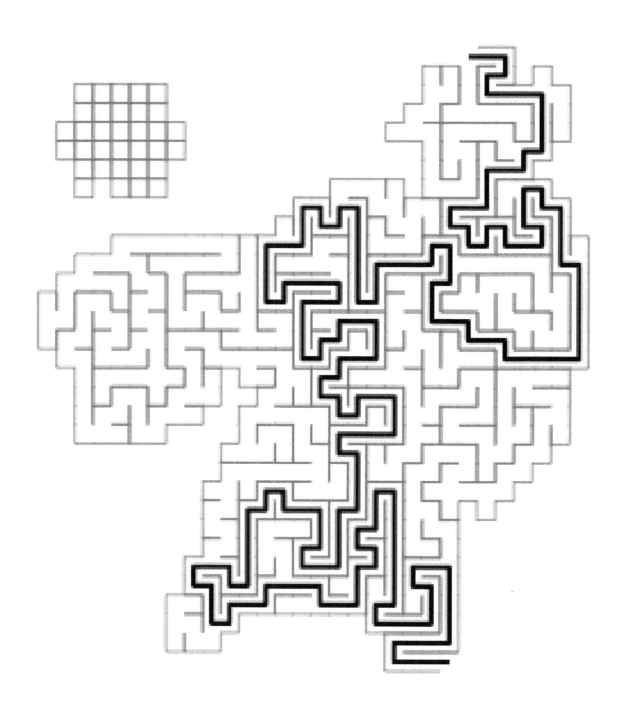

PUZZLE # 31

PUZZLE # 32

PUZZLE # 33

PUZZLE # 34

PUZZLE # 35

PUZZLE # 36

PUZZLE # 37

PUZZLE # 38

PUZZLE # 39

PUZZLE # 40

## How do you like my book?

Please consider leaving a review. I would love to hear your feedback as I am always trying to create better and better books.

**Thank you so much, I truly appreciate it.**

Made in the USA
Las Vegas, NV
02 April 2023

70061900R00050